I Love You Back

(A collection of poems, between her, and he who adores her)

Youssef Khalim

Copyright © 2013 Youssef Khalim

All rights reserved.

ISBN: 978-0-9787798-3-2
ISBN-13: 978-0978779832

DEDICATION

To: Larisa Khalim (The real or ideal soul mate: inspiration)

Tonya Tracy Khalim and

Runako Soyini Khalim, (my most beloved daughters)

Mother and Grandmother and Great-grandmother,
(my most beloved maternal biological ancestors, and spiritual antecedents)

M. A. Garvey (one of my 7 M's: my role models)

Youssef Khalim II; III (my most beloved sons)

Father and Grandfather and Great-grandfather,
(my most beloved paternal biological ancestors, and spiritual antecedents)

To: The Forerunners and Reincarnation sources (beloved biological ancestors and spiritual antecedents), and

The Almighty (our Spiritual Father), from whence we come.

CONTENTS

	Acknowledgments	i
1	Orca	1
2	Orca Too	Pg 2
3	A Long Key	Pg 5
4	You Are The Strongest Wine I Ever Had	Pg 6
5	A Matter of Time	Pg 7
6	Maybe Words May Come	Pg 8
7	Thanks For Coming Out Into My Words	Pg 9
8	Gift	Pg 10
9	Alone At Night	Pg 11
10	Adorable Moments	Pg 12
11	Inspirational Friend	Pg 13
12	You Take Me Everywhere	Pg 14
13	Happy Birthday Gemini	Pg 15
14	I Love You Back	Pg 16
15	What Are We Meeting For This Time?	Pg 19
16	Interesting	Pg 20
17	It' Growing	Pg 21
18	I Had A Dream	Pg 22
19	I Love Spring Practice	Pg 24

20	Teachers' Pet(ting) & Playing	Pg 26
21	She Is The Temple of The Living God	Pg 29
22	Pretty Sweet	Pg 31
23	Your Smile Reminds Me	Pg 32
24	Beloved	Pg 34
25	Blood Lines This Life Time	Pg 35
26	Celebration	Pg 36
27	About the Author, and Other Books	Pg 38

ACKNOWLEDGMENTS

To: The Forerunners and Reincarnation sources
     (beloved biological ancestors and spiritual antecedents), and
     The Almighty (our Spiritual Father), from whence we come.

1 ORCA

Orca, Orca, wild and free,
Come along and swim with me
To a place that we both know
Across the ocean to and fro.

Gliding through the water, we mirror grace,
Sometimes appearing like we're in a race.

Take me on your back, and let me ride with you.
I'll whisper to you, where to take me to.

So, onward to places, I have never been.
Orca, I will always be your friend.

Oh, Orca, beautiful and sweet,
Come along and play with me.
We will frolic in the open sea,
No one can keep you from being free.

I'll play the music you want to hear,
And never again will you live in fear.

I bow to you, Orca:
"King of The Sea"...
And in
My heart you will always be
My secret, and my mystery:
Racing, gliding; wild and free.

2 ORCA TOO

I'd love to see you
Wild and free
To match the spirit of Orca.

So, come with me to the edge
Of the sea
To hitch a ride on Orca.

And you will find
What you want to know
In your going to and fro.

You will be
What you want to be
For, I can see you, truly free.

I'd love to see you
Wild and free
As you are riding Orca:

The ocean mist seen in your hair
Highlights the rainbow that is there.

The sonata you are playing
Sounds much like bands of birds praying.
The "beautiful" that you perceived
Is nothing but your own beauty.

The "sweetness" that you see in Orca
Is nothing but love in your aura.

I'd love to see you
Wild and free
To match the stride of Orca:

I long to see you
Frolic, play
To cool you off in the heat of the day.

I want to see you,

Swim along,
As you remake the ocean home.

He takes you on his back, to ride with you
And you are bound so close, that you are Orca, too.

And then, he takes you places, you both know,
In mountains high above the ocean floor.

And, on to "places, you have never been"
To build a bond that will never end.

He then takes your "bow,"
Turns it into a vow
To always love you.

So, I'd love to see you
Astride; gliding on Orca,
Slashing through the waves,
Leapfrogging through the top soil of the ocean,
Flying, nullifying (embryonic hurricanes)...

Like I was saying:
We must get down
To the edge
Of the sea and
Match the spirit of Orca.

3 A LONG KEY

You are
A key

To my long lost past
And my long-term future
Since I'd spend much too long in the sun to warm me like you do.

It would take too long listening backwards to hear the music your voice speaks.

It would take too long to reach the future without you.

So, long hours with you are
The key.

4 YOU ARE THE STRONGEST WINE I EVER HAD

You must be my dream come true
'Cause in my dreams I drink of you.

You are the strongest wine I ever had,
You drug me with a mighty blast.

And when you give your wine to me
I love to give you mine with glee.

You are the strongest wine I ever had,
Your wine is never, ever bad.

Come on, intoxicate me to the hilt,
I will not care about the guilt.

You are my only drug of choice,
Without your wine I'm simply lost.

I'll surely keep on coming back,
For you my aphrodisiac.

You lift me high to fly in time
Because you are the perfect wine.

I soar above the canyons
With you as my companion.

As long as there is time
I will feast on your wine
And I don't want the rest.

I love it
Need it
Got to have (you).

Forever, forever, forever, forever!
And drink, and drink, and drink, and dream
The strongest wine I ever, ever, ever, ever, had.

5 A MATTER OF TIME

I was sitting here, thinking of you.
There's nothing else I'd rather do.

Thinking of where you might be,
Thinking it's you I want to see.

Thinking of time, that we could share,
Thinking of how I long to be there.

Now, none of this can really be true
'Cause I don't even know you.

Yet, thoughts of you dance through my mind.
I know it's just a matter of time.
But where, and when, will you be mine
When I don't even know you?

You are in my dreams, night and day.
The thoughts never fade away.

How have you made me feel like this?
You make me feel, it's you I miss.

So, I've simply got to know you:
I need to touch your face
Look in your eyes
And feel your heart here next to mine
I want to reach out, and kiss your lips
One kiss for every joy I missed
And keep you dancing through my mind
Day and night, all the time
Wherever, whenever there're thoughts and time

So, I can get to know you.

6 MAYBE WORDS MAY COME

I don't know if this will work.
The words and inspiration do not flow like I am used to.
Let me take leave, to walk within the woods. Then, maybe, words may come.

I'm used to feelings streaming forth as easily as the waters rush the streams in springtime.

Being elated, and writing this in mighty, weighty words that iterate, or move creation.

I'm used to being in love, feeling this response in nature. Then, writing about it.

I'm used to seeing mountains of beauty everywhere. Entering in at every- thing, making my mark, and recording this, in words;

I capture, command, cajole; I even stoop to seducing words, so I can have my way with them.

So, let me take leave, to walk within the woods. Then, maybe, words may come.

7 THANKS FOR COMING OUT INTO MY WORDS

The words are formed within (my soul), by you.
Then, I feel you in my heart,
A part, of me.

And I want to love
The part of you
Within me,
Outside me,
Wherever you are.

I reach in to you, out to you
Wherever you are

To say: I love you, love you
Love you: wonderful (lovely-exotic-beauty).

And, I want you, want you, want you, in my words, forevermore.

I really do love - you

And my love is reaching out.
For, without a doubt, I love you.
And throughout my being
There is one accord
It's just one word:
And, I love you, love you, love you
And my heart says, "Yes!"

"That's what life is all about."
So, thanks for coming out, into my words.

8 GIFT

I have one more gift
For you,
Which is actually a gift
From you,
Making it a gift from both to each.

When used,
It makes us richer,
Makes us happy
Gets better
And Multiplies;
(& my gift)
Awaits your use.

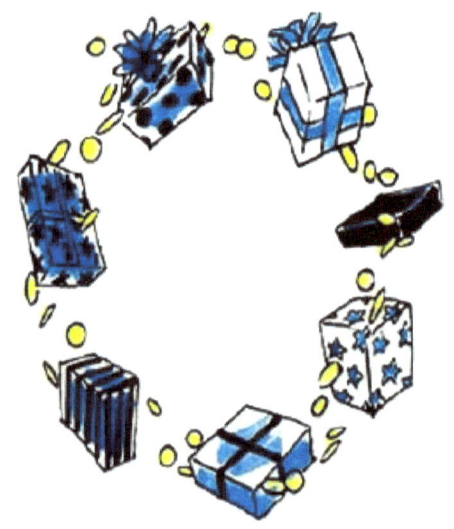

9 ALONE AT NIGHT

You can come and set me free
If you come here, next to me.

We can soar to lofty heights
Like an arrow takes to flight.

And the day we are together
Is when we feel what lasts forever.

And sure as gold will never perish
We build a love, you'll want to cherish.

And as a rose perfumes the air
Our love will freshen everywhere.

And being alone at night will vanish
Banished by the light of love.

So, come along, and set me free
And get your love, here next to me.

10 ADORABLE MOMENTS

I absolutely
And thoroughly
Adore
The stunningly beautiful
And Considerate
And lovable
Moments
(You) Create.

11 INSPIRATIONAL FRIEND

To my very special friend
Whose
Beauty & presence
Rekindles in me
The
Powerful forces of
Love &
Inspiration
Motivation
Desire
& life.

12 YOU TAKE ME EVERYWHERE

When I'm with you, you take me everywhere.
I want to go with you to there (now).

Say, where have you been?
Come, give my world a spin.

You send my soul to singing.
You give my life its meaning.

I love to be with you.
You touch me through and through.

I love the way you smile.
Come, send me for a while.

I want you back, here today.
Is this new position OK?

The love you give has set me free.
You show me more, what love can be.

Come, take me everywhere.
Come, and take me there.

13 HAPPY BIRTHDAY GEMINI

Happy Birthday Gemini!
I can't wait
To see and celebrate you
Today, tomorrow, next week, next month, next year, Post-time
(If it's when time is real).

You're getting better every year:
Your lips are sweeter
Your laughter richer

Your wisdom keeps on growing,
Your eyes reflect the spring times truer.

You warm me when I think of you,
When you come near,
I'm set ablaze into a steady flame.

I can't wait
To hold you
Taste you
Hear you in my ear
And love the very thought of you
Today, tomorrow, next week, next month, next year, Post-time
(If it's when
Time is real).

14 I LOVE YOU BACK

She smiled and said, "Hello!"
He said, "How are you?"
"Fine."
"I'll say!"
He said, "You know, I have the biggest crush on you."
She said, "Why is that?"
He said, "It's because of the way you laugh."
"Are you serious?"
He said, "You have a deep, full laugh. That's the kind of laugh I can warm up to."
"So, you like me for my laugh?"
"I adore you because you're bright, lovely; you're natural. You talk, you walk; you think, and act like a free person would do."
"Are you trying to say, 'Healthy'?"
"In one word, maybe.'"
"And you've been telling me that you're in love with me?"
"When I see or think of you, I love you. And every time I see you, I love you all over again."
She said, "Sometimes I love you much too much. That kind of love can get you hurt. I care so much, and want you so. These things I tell, you shouldn't know. Your love may be just like the rest: Take all my love, and move your nest."
He said, "Why do you love me?"
"Because you're special."
"What?"
"You're nice."
"Hmmmm," he said.
And then she said, "You have reminded me of 'Dr. J'"
" He said, "Yes, but I can't fly."
"Or, maybe, Billy Dee Williams."

"Well, my acting is for real."

"Ah ha!" She said. "You remind me of Andre Dawson. You know, he used to play with the 'Cubs.' Have you been working out?"

"Well, I do...'Love Spring Practice'. But I have to work on hitting home runs."

Then he said, "I love to score with you anytime."

She said, "We make an interesting team."

"A winning team," he reminded her.

She said, "You know, you're using me to produce words for you."

"No, I'm using you to make me whole, so that we can be productive."

"When will this end?"

When we curl up time to bed,
And lifetime after lifetime is no more.

And I have no heart to adore you with, No
arms to reach for you,
No words to say, "I love you" with;

When we reclaim the earth, And
make a better way.

And love is seen in all its Glory,
And creates a better day.

And when we fully

Preach His word.
And redeem His chosen and His good;

When I no longer need
To practice loving fully.

And when we all can say to Him
Like I now say to you:

"Thanks for loving me
Throughout eternity.

With all the Force and Power of the universe
I love you back, fully, forever; I love you,
I truly love you back!"

I Love You
Back.

15 WHAT ARE WE MEETING FOR THIS TIME?

Because I love you
I want from you
The time to
Meet,
To give to you
Everything
Or nothing
Or something in between
For a moment
Or an hour
Of one day
Of one lifetime
For all eternity.

I'll give you
So much more
Than hours have to give,
So let's consider days...
And if you plan for just
One day
That plan won't bother me
For you'll be back
We'll find a way
Throughout the span of time.

Because I love you
Endlessly
I know just how to give you

Everything into
One day
To make this life complete.

And you'll be back
Throughout all time
We'll meet, we'll meet
We'll meet.

16 INTERESTING…

The most interesting
Things about you
(Not necessarily in that order), are:

Your intelligence
(Knowledge and knowing)

Your freckles; and your hair
(I love your freckles, and to see your hair in sunlight)

Your laugh, smiles, and sense of humor
(You have the best Illinois, land of Lincoln, world-class, classic, sunny smile)

Your eyes
(Forgive me if I stare at you)

Your voice
(I love to hear you talk; or just say wisdom words)

And
Your body
(Yes!!)

But… the most interesting
Things about you are:
Your interests
(And their order).

17 IT'S GROWING

My love for you is growing
Just as newly forming
Mountains seek the sky.

In time
These towering powerhouses
And our heaven
Meet.

18 I HAD A DREAM

Who is this man, this man I see
Who comes and visits in my sleep?

He stands there looking over me
As if he knows just what I seek.

He must know me secretly
Because he knows me in my sleep.

You know, this man is always there.
Somehow, he knows me everywhere.

He reaches out and touches me:
A perfect date with destiny.

Hand in hand, we take a walk,
And laugh and talk like lovers talk.

There is a soft and gentle breeze,
And songs of birds are heard from trees.

The sun is shining in our face;
Our glow of love will never fade.

He looks into my eyes,
Stirring feelings deep inside.

Then, he holds me in his arms
For a kiss that you would miss.

Then, the man knows what to do:
He takes, and loves me through and through.

And when I know we'll never part,
I awaken with a start!

Now is my life a fantasy
Because I'd rather be asleep?

Who is this man, this man I see
Who comes and visits in my sleep?

I suspect that it is you,
Because my dreams always come true.

19 I LOVE SPRING PRACTICE

I like to practice making love with you.
I send it into you
As our eyes meet
As our hands touch
And as we talk.

I go for the goal: as long distance lover.
I pump it up for hours
& into you
'Cross time and space:
I love you when I think of you
I telegraph it, phone it, write it, speak it, spout it!
(I almost shout it).
Then calm me, warm me down.

Not just for our coming acrobatic ecstatic interlude, but
For the long season of life ahead,
I change my pace & perform the following exercise:

I name a cloud for you,
And taste you in every drop of water from the sky.

I write a song for you
For broadcast over satellite

To the endless universe:
Your fame will never end.

I wish you God speed, joy and happiness,
And bid you meet the heavenly hosts and benefactors.

I send so much love to you that
It makes a visible path in the invisible skies.

And finally, I wrap you in my aura
So you can see forever.

Now this love workout is so good to us
And good for us,
& when you come off the sidelines &
Do it with me,
We'll both be
Fit & Trim.

20 TEACHERS PET(TING) & PLAYING

Because I need to grow
It's you I need to know.

To learn the hidden facts
We need to interact.

Because we all can teach,
We all can bridge the breech.

I'll be your teacher's pet,
So ask, & see what you can get.

We'll study what's old, and study what's new,
And why I love you (when there is no clue).

We'll get at why I share, and care for you,
And why in the world there's morning dew.

Together we both can ponder
What's in here, and what's out yonder.

We'll look at how the earth was born,
And find the path to where it's going.

We'll find out why you are a lovely star,
& snowflakes are the way they are.

And why I love you without end,
And it rains on oceans when it is sent.

We'll study and pass the hardest test,
Know when and where the sun star rests.

And why you look and taste so sweet,
And intersections tend to meet.

And to love you once is not enough,
And penguins walk to strut their stuff.

And why tomorrow always comes,
And we can't put off what happened once.

Why good people sometimes act so bad,
And whatever is made, can never last.

We'll look at everlasting love and joy,
And maybe our firstborn will be a boy.

Why we shed tears when we feel so good,
And I'd be with you if I only could.

Why loving you is so much fun,
And why a fire will make things burn.

And why our children are so bright,
And confirm that God is made of Light.

We'll find out who & what we are today,
And why our forefathers taught us to pray.

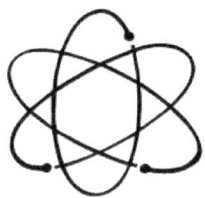

Why loving you is what I need,
And plants and animals need to feed.

Our field trip will take you
Where you have the nerve to go.

And I will surely love you
Round your every curve & more.

And find the bustling play lot
Where angels like to play,
Learn how to bathe in Father's Glory
'Til night turns into day.

We should not wait or hesitate.
Together we both can graduate.

Because (we need to know),
In love, we both can grow.

21 SHE IS THE TEMPLE OF THE LIVING GOD

She is the Temple of The Living God;
An apparel, adornment for him.
So, go ahead, adore and love her
Sharing all you have.

And he is The Temple of The Living God.
An apparel, adornment for her.
So, share your all with him.

Then, fight for love, in the world:

Go, love a Mormon, Muslim, Jew, Hindu, Sikh, Buddhist, Adventist, "Witness."

Love an American today. Then, love an Asian, an African, a European.

Go, love a Native American. And don't stop there.

Even, love an atheist, materialist, the selfish (they need a lot of love).

Then, wage a *Holy War Of Love*:
Of caring, sharing,
And daring Adorations.

Adopt *The Declaration of Love*. Complete *Our Spiritual Revolution*
And overthrow the evil devils.

Get Independent.
Adore the Origin of Love (inside, outside).
He resides in everyone (and out there).

Then, get eternal, universal citizenship,
And care, and share
With daring adorations
Of The Temple of God.

22 PRETTY SWEET

You are
Pretty sweet,
Refreshingly sweet,
Wonderful,
Delicious,
Candy sweet,
& pretty.

23 YOUR SMILE REMINDS ME

Your smile reminds me of
The wondrous phases of life:
The omnipresent green of spring,
Or wintry, snowy white;
The smell of leafy, ruffled, multicolored leaves of fall;

The travels in His Will & Might;
Breathing life in all the seasons,
Planting roots in matter,
Where bounds do not exist.

The vistas in your smiling eyes
Enhance your lips with nectar, dew
And everlasting Light
Must live securely in you.

Your smile reminds me of the need
To know you: See the blueprint,
Touch the very foundations,

And build that Beauty, and the Majesty
That we have known, and that you smile.

Your smile reminds me of all joys;
Of perfect love, and welcome time

(When peace is born),
And all creation smiles.

24 BELOVED

(*Beloved* is the meaning of Amy)

The wonderful word that
One can say
Is
She:

Her smile will set your Chakras spinning
The angels named her
Thus:
Beloved.

Our God has called her
Splendid radiance, and priceless princess;
Adored before time was, until it ceases.

Can any look as sweet & lovely?
Her mission: "man's most pleasing form of life."

Can any word(s)
"Be-loved" as dearly
As this wonderful
She?

25 BLOOD LINES THIS LIFE TIME

I'm happy to renew
My acquaintance with you
From that lifetime.

I love to (love you) to
Pick up the conversation
Where we left off before

So, we can renew
My blood line with your blood line
For all times.

26 CELEBRATION

I serenade you on this date
To still the music you generate,

And celebrate you in this way,
The beauty in my dreams & fate.

The lines will last forever more
To show it's you that I adore.

So, here is my pledge made to you.
It's clear to me what I shall do:

Think of you on every morning
Pretty birds sing pretty songs.

Rename Venus after you,
& call its moons our children's names.

Give my heart adorned with love,
To share the powers of our minds.

Plant flowers in the spring
That show the rainbows of our love.

Write words of you that build
A spiral staircase in the skies.

Wrap you in apparels of our love
To keep your heart both warm and kind.

Reclaim the earth, recapture time;
And give you some, & give you some.

And travel endless love with you
Until we find the end.

And serenade you, celebrate you
One time past that when.

Then celebrate you, celebrate you
Again, & again, and again.

27 ABOUT THE AUTHOR, AND OTHER BOOKS

Youssef Khalim obtained Unity in yoga on about 7/20/80. He says, "we will recombine into one faith, Judaism, Christianity, and Islam." He has been able to "see" and experience some amazing information about USA presidents Jefferson, Lincoln, and Obama; and also Prophets Moses, Muhammad, and Solomon - in visions, lucid dreams, and in meditation. Khalim makes reincarnation (resurrection) central again in our western religions. He resides in the Chicagoland area. And he is the father of Tonya, Runako, and Noah. His books are available at: http://amazon.com, http://sunracommunications.com and http://lulu.com

Youssef Khalim's books include *People Of The Future/Day; You Are Too Beautiful; The Resurrection of Noah; You Look So Good; Healing Begins With The Mind; Jubilee Worldwide; Lara, Forever; Tanisha Love; Galina, All About Love; I Call My Sugar, Candie; Natalia, With Love; Svetlana, Angel Of Love; Lori, My Dream Girl*; *Love of My Life*; and *The Second Coming*.

www.ingramcontent.com/pod-product-compliance
Lightning Source LLC
Chambersburg PA
CBHW042324150426
43192CB00001B/38